LAKES AND GARDENS

poems

Hannie Rouweler

Demer Press

for my daughter

Publisher: Demer Press, Belgium

First edition: 2008
Second edition: 2010

ISBN: 978-90-9022797-9

Translations by John Irons
and Hannie Rouweler

LAKES AND GARDENS

Demer Press

INDEX

Dream, water

Hills, borders

Echoes, voices

Church bells, words

List of translations made by John Irons:

Woman I, II, III, Between times, Bits and Pieces, Breathless asymmetry, Crossroads, Daughters, Homecoming, India, Melly's, Killybegs, Memory of my mother, No Muse, On a rose, Cows, White boat, Banjo, Fox, Friend in Scotland, Father, The recurrence of things, Eye test, Night ride, Oneness, At a coast, Present, Free notes, Requiem for words, A word in a star, Sun in branches, Robin in Pearse's garden, Black lover.

DREAM, WATER

BY CONTRACT
(love certificate for a translator)

In each sentence a word is overboard
while I'm translating the signs from the North

in a barrel. To save.
What's good, you put aside. You don't burn it up,

it goes in a bottle for the beach walker.
You start a conversation, and let your hand

glide over my shoulder. To the navel.
I'm reading further feverishly, as so much more

has to be recorded, bent to all directions, on paper.
While outside bare branches lose themselves

in gusts of wind, a bird rages by,
and leaves let themselves be shaken up and divided

like a pack of cards. For each one a piece of time,
half a sea, a handful of love and death, and that's it

for today. I haven't yet finished my work.
You've got to come back if you stay, really want me.

PHOTO

A boy
is holding a violin

the beginning of a trembling, tender
string to a steady voice is already heard

in the room
we left in all our yesterdays.

A boy is listening to his imagination
in rough colours of dawn

morning light. We follow the path
beyond borders and limited time

and see in black and white more clearly
the truth of memory, just for a moment,

an angle in the distance. And waiting for
bunnies (Easter), angels (Christmas) is

one of the dreams never passing by. In
old instruments, even Bach's compositions

there's no beginning, no end.
We know how it is to be a child.

Woman I

DREAM,
WATER

you will not find her
in the street
she will elude you

in every face
of a young woman
who laughs at you
stretches out a hand.

you'll feel just for an instant
that you knew her
as the girl from yesterday
that you loved.

she's already vanished in the mirror
called recollection
with her full round mouth
dark eyes

that touched your soul
for this moment:
the longing
that never passes.

Woman II

FRUIT,
EARTH

she will always be there
even though she lives concealed
in a garden

where you thought
to find her skin,
the outpouring
in her declaration of love.

the sunlight that slides
over her body
betrays time,
a hand protects.

she returns
if you know her real name,
be silent then and let her
stand in silence

by the fountain: live
in the deepest sense
towards a climax
of love for ever.

Woman III

THE FALL,
PARADISE

in her hand she
is still holding
the apple

but who has the courage
to refuse
a fruit
in freedom and love?

she is the first woman
never to have covered
her nakedness,
in her open gaze

no doubts,
revenge she does not know
in rejection and deception,
in tear-filled eyes

lies the truth: loss,
the lie of the serpent,
the paradise without angels,
broken-winged she worships the man.

(three poems at pictures
by Willy Vanheers)

ANN'S PORCH
(Florida)

A palm tree on the other side of
water streaming along and along.
A blue sky,
couple of birds floating in the air,
old oak trees
dropping their large shadows on grass.

Empty clothes lines with pins
dancing lucidly in the wind.
Beside a stone wall
Bougainville growing for years
suddenly turned from pink to dark purple
on one particular day, she said.

A hand pours coffee into my cup:
'I never liked the white flowers
my dad gave to me when I was a child'.

Is this an early morning full of joy
just for being there? Is this another day,
or is this just forever? Forever?

BETWEEN TIMES

for John Irons

It makes you milder, old age,
sorrow too. You don't break your teeth

on words any more. You don't
run on ahead any longer with all sorts

of ideas. You don't run after
the facts either. Much you let be,

you grow milder. You live more
by your emotions and what

things signify. Everything is
best translated in images,

views, a young flower in
the garden. Your hair grows thin, grey

and photos are framed more often.
You keep what you never want to lose.

BITS AND PIECES

Spring and summer –

We lie in the grass.
We look at clouds.

We're girls in our white dresses
with coloured bows in our hair.

I walk hand in hand with you in the meadows
of Goor and the hills of Grisdale. We pick

flowers for our mothers. Whitsun flowers.
Mothers always put flowers from their daughters

in a vase, even though wild flowers soon droop
over the rim after three days, their stems pliant.

We scratch a hopscotch court with a stick.
You put some sand in a tin and I push it to the edge.

Autumn and winter –

The leaves turn russet in the woods of the
Olympic Mountains and yellowish-brown in de Kempen.

We look for edible mushrooms. You know exactly which
are poisonous or inedible. I trust you blindly.

We have already had many lives and each brought light
and darkness. Love has been the broadest path

that sometimes narrowed into an alley, a water
in which feelings drowned and later resurfaced.

The bare trunks of the trees know their history.
A new branch grows when one got broken off and never

returned. We take trains and ferries to the far side,
remember the faces of the dead. Their words

nourish the soil. The compost of time, fertile
as valleys of sadness and memory. We recall everything

and forget what's better forgotten. The poison evaporates.
Your echo floats gleaming like a white lily in a flurry of snow.

(for Tess Gallagher)

BREATHLESS ASYMMETRY

Why though always that panting,
that sweet panting in poetry,
dear poet, if you give language
its own breath
in the chest
or close to the heart
the soft coursing of
blood through veins
the opening and closing
of words
in rhythmic action
of sounds as in a sonata
the lift-off of sea birds
from rocks
the disappearance of light
behind trees
until the moon rises,
the deer appears
in an open glade.
Ah then, dearest poet,
then it is still early enough
to move more quickly, hunted
up hill and down dale
after the game that
hides in the covert.
Deeper and farther off
the real panting begins
if you no longer return
to your origin, close to water
in a womb, in silence
before your first cry.

(for Albert Hagenaars)

CROSSROADS

When the hour has come
that must move on,
that falls over boundaries
and sails into the distance

the hour has also come
that stands motionless
between two times,
and on recurring reconsiders.

That is the moment
to go away
and to arrive elsewhere.

DAUGHTERS

I look at their slender fingers, where I once could see great silver
rings that are missing on both hands. They are so alike, so like each
other, with the same dark shoulder-length hair, sometimes the same
look in their eyes, eyes of nineteen-year-old girls. I still don't know
them well, I never sat opposite them at table and only now see that
the one holds her knife in the right hand, the other in the left.
They cut through a piece of meat, they take hold of a glass.

Their hands are so slender, and fragile and strong that I hear them
playing Schubert, Beethoven, Chopin in the hall where whole rows of
families share tables, walk over to the buffet, talk about this, that and
the other. A grandma joins in the conversation, an aunt comes now and
then to forge links, to let a familiar voice be heard. They nod with their
heads.
I see them at a harp, hear music in their silence, their language strikes
up like a string quartet, in the street, only for chance passers-by.

I will never be able to forget them, as they are now, and so plentifully
for and with each other. And next to them sits their father.
He glances at them from time to time. He only says dear, intimate
things, nothing about their beautiful hands.
I would like to say how much I love him when I look at his
daughters, as they are together.
How much hidden music lies concealed in hands.

(for Frauke and Bregje)

DUBLIN

We lay on a bed
in the afternoon with yellow sparkling beams of light
streaming into the hotel room.
We lay in each other's arms
and blew each other's dreams and breath
to each other's face
                    till we fell asleep.

And the light vanished and came back
in dark spots before my eyes
as I sank away in all the loves which came together
earlier in time
in a bed
                    along a seashore.

I thought of him and his stories about a woman
he loved and left
in the streets of Dublin.
I thought of him, who I left at a door
in a deserted village.

I wanted to wake you up,
the one who was lying beside me to say
that I always will stay.

So many other things I wanted to say to you
but I touched your mouth
kissed your lips
in which silence drifted away to basalt blocks
along the bay.
             I would love you forever.

Always we would remember the towers
in which the most beautiful words are preserved.

EMPTINESS
(on Iceland)

I shrank back for
such untroubled emptiness
and deep desolation
as if she had turned away
from everyone for ages

a lonely, far away star
in the nocturnal firmament.

But in the transparency of lines
in the wide and open landscape
bending and arising into
unknown places at a distance
I saw the wild forces of her nature
untamed like a herd of horses on the run.

GREEN GRASS

Lectori Salutem

I've read so many words
in books
in trains
and planes
in countries
in rosebuds
and
in gardens
in faces
of women and men.
So many words I've read
about love
about pain
loss
and desire.
The past often nearby.
I am a stranger, however,
absent and remote
in all your paperwork.
And I don't complain.
WHY?
We all are lonely
in the end
and only few bear in mind
who these splendid words
were meant for:
We look in maps and cards
and hardly know
which lovers ever lived
in all these poets' hearts.

TREES IN THE WINDOW

The trees in my window
are not that old
they may last many more years –
and carry the wind
from the land to the sea.

They are poplars in a long row
(called 'pepples' in Flanders)
and exist over thirty years
(according to my husband born
100 yards from here, in this village)
and I've seen with my own eyes
that they overcome each storm –
only now and then a branch breaks down.

The branches of the tree in your window
reach to heaven,
and at night when you stand on your balcony
watching stars, space and time,
their arms are long
and strong and make a victory sign
peace,
always peace,
nothing but peace.

Our trees will never forget each other.
They know you saw them, every day,
and that I never would leave this place,
their thick leaves in Spring
will safe-guard our dreams and memories.

(for Leo and Tineke Vroman)

HILLS, BORDERS

HOMECOMING

This morning I got up with my father's voice:
don't put such a short skirt on,
it makes things really easy for the lads.
My father lays aside his paper and observes

me combing my long hair before the mirror,
tracing my eyelids with a thick eyeliner.
I'd never had this short and taut a mini-skirt.

Once more my father, on the sofa, plus cigar
and in his aged eyes now only questions:
pour me some coffee, make me a sandwich
in his helplessness sound like orders.

I'd heard those orders before – a man always wants
coffee, always food on the table, a man always wants
a woman in the car, in bed.
I'm home again in ten marriages at once
and bless this day. Today I'm free.

HOW IS SHE DOING

Today? How is Barbara doing? As I remember
she ran half a marathon with a friend
and didn't come back. When she left this morning
I heard her steps on the stairway and a door shut
before I could say a word in my sleep.
We drank coffee in a restaurant after breakfast,
went to a bookstore and sat in the garden.
We watched cats and TV. I was reading poems and
wrote a poem myself. Forgot about the words.
I had some difficulty to get it printed on paper
as I couldn't find a printer in this home.
My poem is drifting away in a program
I didn't fix myself. Have to look it up later.
I remember Barbara as a woman with blond hair,
pleasant features, long legs, with an easygoing smile
on her face. A Greek goddess like in old paintings.
How is Barbara doing today?
I wonder if she will ever know how worried I am, about
how things will be after midnight. I wait for her steps,
a sign, a car that drives up to the hills and a lake
in which we live with the sounds of the birds,
a sunset and light over water, in a safe house for all.

HOUSE ON THE HILL

There was a house I once lived in
with huge windows
over viewing hills until borders of the sea
suddenly it cracked
pieces of glass fell on the floor

I'll go there no more
I'll go there no more
I can't see it anymore
I can't see it anymore
I won't hear it anymore.

All parts of glass and dreams and hopes
as fallen from the hands of a drunken man
and his drunken droopsy dradsy words
are not to be collected anymore –
- not to be remembered anymore -
it only cuts deep wounds
in the eyes of a believer,
in the ears of the truth never to be heard.

Only straight thoughts keep me clear and clean
today
though in mirrors I see one face behind the other
never mine
waiting for the wolf or fox
its nightly attacks in the dark without moon.

Soon I'll wake up in another dawn,
don't know when –
windows overlooking long branches filled with apples
just to be picked up.
To hold happiness in your hand, simple as that,
like the good life can be in the sun, a garden,
on a bright day in July.

FROM BRUSSELS
(with love)

You come from Brussels.
You've parked your car in Hasselt
and took the train.
You went by train to avoid
the traffic on the highway to Antwerp
during the rush hour.

You could have come from any city
    walking
    biking
    hitch hiking
I would have been here anyway.

I come from my bedroom
went to the living room
went straight to the kitchen
to drink milk, make coffee

I took a piece of cake
a book
checked the mail to see if there was
anything special in it for me
I wrote a poem
to prevent a collision of mornings
and afternoons,
to make sense to all the ways
of unseen things

a bird in my garden
a cloud passing by
a cat on the lawn
a tree shaking his leaves

which do happen during the day
when you pay attention.

INDIA

for Sujata Bhatt

You start your letters with dotted lines between
the words and I see there an indescribable space.
It is as if you had forgotten something, as if you wanted to say
something I didn't know. Are they the white transition areas,
boundaries that we pass in our everyday lives
from one person to another? Or are they white spots
in the memory, like the picture you have of your mother
when she was younger and later as an old woman
dredges up memories from earlier years that could
never have been yours?
My youth was a garden, a vegetable garden with lettuce and
green beans. Father built houses and smelled of
cement and his work-clothes were covered in white spots.
My mother's kitchen smelled of boiled
potatoes, beetroots, cabbage, sausage.
May I therefore ask you to take me with you to
Poona? To the places of your youth, the house of your
grandmother where we walk together in the monsoon
rains, pick up a snake, stroke
a lion, cherish the warm bodies of fat apes?
Teach me to see nature with your eyes,
the rising of the sun, the disappearing of
a person in the crowd, being alone at evening,
listening to birds, sounds in the night.
Open the windows to a door that is open for you,
in the valleys of the area where I live, the woods
and the Kempen, the house that I share with my husband
in a suburb, a field, the view of a row of
trees behind which sheep and horses graze.

Sleep in the bed that you occupy, occupied in your dreams.
On the wall hang paintings and poems
behind glass about love, loss, death.
Use the bath, the mirror, the towels and comb
your hair, take care of your skin so as to find again your face
in traces memories that you left behind to catch a train
to Brussels. Teach me to see with your eyes, to read
with your memory full of coloured and white images
of your youth in India, the break, life between two parts
of the world and oceans and see the banks of holy
rivers, waterfalls, small streams through a valley.
Behind lies history in a crumbled story in which
we create language that we ourselves change into sounds,
the rhythm of the dark, the rhythm of the light.
Like the music of Bach, Beethoven, Mozart.

RED AND WHITE (1894)

Edvard Munch

What didn't have a future always had
a past.
Even in serene outlooks on sea-shores or
riverbanks.
Skies, birds flying, clouds.

At this crossing two women met looking away
from the other side of the same mirror.
Dressed in white and red.

Standing on the same spot the painter
put them in the picture together
like two forlorn sisters unwillingly
belonging to one another.
In the darkness of a background painfully
filled with death, and hope.

So much more alive they are now, and present
in themselves as if they had turned into
sphinxes, standing forever at the entrance
of an imagined, unknown door
leading to unguarded secrets.
Maybe to paradise.

An eternal separation of minds
falls over their beautiful long skirts.

From: "A timeless tide"
(2001)

LISTENING TO SIBELIUS

Whereas I was listening to Sibelius
I was thinking of you
there Up in the North close to
the North Pole
(Iceland, Canada, Alaska)
so far away from us
and I was happy
to learn
from a local newspaper
down here
in the heart of wetlands
that the average rate of
suicide went down,
people drink less alcohol (vodka)
(like here)
seem to be more content,
as we really should concern ourselves
more
about dark countries (Africa)
poor children (Far East)
than the dark part in ourselves.
And I was happy to learn
that what I thought
or wrote
to a very dear friend of mine
could go for myself as well
(if I really tried harder
to stand in someone else's
footsteps).
In the music of Sibelius
one can drift away
along all coasts of love,
nature,
and the lakes will do the rest.

MELLY'S, KILLYBEGS

From this window I see her walk along the quay
with fishing boats beneath a cloudy Irish sky

to the strand further on, past boulders wildly
and savagely pounded by the sea on rough days.

There she sought rest, quietness for herself, according
to Patricia the pensioner, who knew her since school.

Rest she found nowhere again, nor peace
with herself. We opened the cemetery gate

and looked for her name on old and new gravestones,
laid out on a hillside overlooking a lake.

Everywhere I found pain, everywhere it pricked me
like thistles underfoot. Everywhere I loved her.

Whatever might be said of her, now or later,
had no effect on me. She was good as she was,

she was good for me in all her despair, words
of love for her surroundings, until her death.

The 12.25 bus for Donegal will soon be leaving.
I've one hour left, the time of the death throes

of a dog, as she writes in one of her poems.
An hour to drink coffee beside the window

to still be with her and Irish light between
dark clouds of sadness and oblivion.

(in memory of Noelle Vial)

MEMORY OF MY MOTHER

Ever more days grow between you
and me since you left for good that late afternoon,
unannounced, with no farewell,
without an image to hold on to

as a last memory, sign of life.
Then everything began to waver, wander
with me unable to see a hand in front of my face.
Later light came when someone spoke of you.

Then I saw you opposite me on a chair or walking
from room to kitchen. We never had
a good conversation, not your style, we lived
in sign language. A look from you sufficed.

Three words was what I heard and all else flew out
the window towards my freedom. I loved you most
as a mother without language, silent,
I only recall you as a presence, a shadow in the

distance, evening light above long-gone fields of my youth.
Give me back your breath, the gentle hands on my
shoulder, the quick kiss of a departure that returns
when I close my weary eyes or dream this is how it will be.

MINOR KEY

for Charles Simic

The minor key is the only key
to freedom, freedom of speech

but I lost it in my youth.
I know it's somewhere

maybe in my piano.
I once bought a piano named Fazer

Finnish, small and black.
My mother sent me to piano lessons

when I was a child. I'm stuck with it.
My brother complains - he is over

60: I haven't had any education.
I say: I agree, but no one has shown me

the key I lost one day. It should be
in an old coat or in someone's attic

as all things gone are hidden in
safe places you never thought about.

MUSIC

With you I've spent most of my days
Beethoven

you were never there. You were on a picture,
an old man, grey, deaf

and in your features I meant to see something
of all the slowly increasing, heavy

sounds, I lived with day and night.
I know you better in all your rehearsals

(hearing again and again, listening anew to what's
coming to me) than anyone or anything else.

In the rhythm of the light, gravity, beyond borders.
Even in my sleep, my uncatchable dreams

I feel a vague presence which will never leave me
in its deepest ground. You'll always be there, in any shape.

NO MUSE

Although I am no muse on silent feet
I lie in the flatlands of my dreams
on a coast far from here

and watch the clouds drift past
towards shores that caress me, let my hair
flutter in the wind of longing

towards silence, sweet floors. Although I know
I cannot be more for you than a word
among hundreds printed in a sentence

where everything is divided into what exists:
I recall you in a name, a thing,
a lasting current of life that does not disappear.

So be off with your imaginings of non-
existent women or who took you too briefly
by the hand and dragged you off to an abyss.

Just call me the North Star once more,
Princess of the Wadden Sea, and I love the earth,
the mudflats and the water that washed over me.

ON A ROSE

It is
exceptionally

quite exceptionally
beautiful.

Comparable
with nothing

only: dawn breaking
above a blue coastline

sunlight against
a mountain ridge, volcano.

It is
sun

water
red

blossom
shadow.

PERSPECTIVE

Like a tree is dependent
of the strength of its roots,
we scan endurance
in time, happiness and light.

As we grow older
language seems more vulnerable,
half words are enough
to grasp it all.

Again we become children
and reduce words
which have been bigger
than ourselves.

PLAYING GROUNDS

Daddy is saying

Do you want me up?
Do you want me down?

Daddy is saying
Up?
Or down?

I hear daddy saying
It's okay

Daddy says
Fine

Daddy says
I'll do what you like

* sweet conversation between father and child
that I overheard in a garden

POETRY

Look, this is poetry –
I said to a friend.
The tree with countless yellow leaves
standing in front of our window.

The stem is the shape, structure,
leaves are the words, contents,
they fall down in Autumn
and bare branches are remnants.

The tree is on its own among other trees,
the wood is big, the paths lie concealed
and we are looking, don't know for what.
A poem is light, and searching and wandering.

PRAYER

Dear God,

Creator of the Universe,

most original Inventor and Artist
in the world,
(after him a long time nothing,
then Leonardo Da Vinci)

best Painter,
(after him a long time nothing,
then Vincent van Gogh)

best Poet,
(after him a long time nothing,
then Leo Vroman)

Please – give me
a bit,

just a little bit.

I've just returned from Italy.

LANGUAGE END

Language stood like a scythe
at my door

he asked whether the grass
grew high in my garden
or the hedge had to be cut
or trees pruned

he glanced inside
with green eyes.

I said that in my garden
violets flowered abundantly
and that the wild grass with worms
was meant for birds.

He asked if there were still other odd jobs
to be done
and scanned my neck
with his eye.

Go to my neighbours
or around the block – I shouted

old goatwoolsockknitter
typhuspoxtropicalmalariasmuggler

and slammed the door in his face.

Afterwards I wrote a poem
I felt an enormous relief.

(for Gerrit Komrij)

ECHOES, VOICES

COWS

Today I feel an irrepressible urge
to write about cows

I see them every day
grazing in a meadow behind this neighbourhood

and it's always the same cows:
two with a blaze and two whites.

I want to have a good think about cows,
what sort of animals are they and what's their purpose

here on earth? To be happy, like us?
And what about the next life, once they're

no longer there in the meadow? Do I get it wrong
and mistake other cows for these ones?

I want to solve this problem today.
I've no time for nonsense, stupid questions

that never have an answer. I've enough time
to think about one single thing. For according

to some philosophers you suss much more
when you compare one thing with 1001 others.

RHYME

I was sitting in a café
the other day
with a pen
in my hand
and a mirror at my back
on the table
there stood a cup of coffee
and a spoon
white paper and I looked around
some people
looked at me and I was wondering
if this was as I was alone or
because I had a pen in my hand.
The first line
was easily written
I had something (somebody) in my mind
by which I got started right away.
The second line
came with some effort
as there was no sunshine in my window
only a cloudy day and no one outside
seemed to care what I was doing.
The third line
was even worse with a heavy sigh
as I had to let go the person
in my first line and nothing
showed up instead of him.
Just at the moment I wanted
to give up this all
the waiter passed and asked
can I be of any service, madam?
I said: yes.
Finish my poem.
I wrote a poem in one breath
over the hills of memory.

SHORT POEMS

1.

He jumps up
the poet's soul
until he goes down

Deep in the water, unseen,
like me - I lie on the bottom
of the ocean

Waiting for the following push-up.

2.

Look at the splendour
when they all jump up
together

It's as if an unknown conductor gives
the sign to all musicians
to start the orchestra at once

Jumping dolphins in a group
is the best Opera
ever seen.

3.

How sweet the little one
beside his mother,
she surely keeps an eye on him

For predators -
there's always some danger
in an ocean like everywhere else

We should save the old secrets
of animals having their own language:
their sounds are echoes
of our voices.

4.

We can swim with them, we can
feel a lot better
being in touch with them
than trust our own instincts and beliefs

Dolphins have a knowledge of being
we almost forgot
just being, the way you are, the way

I am
acceptance of pain and loss -
in their brightness they bring back
peace to the world.

5.

Let me dream again of places
I have been long ago
along a turbulent coast

And see them again:
dolphins jumping up in the air
touching the heavens of delight

Like fountains of love
we remember our loves.

(at Paintings of Dolphins
by Evelyn Chan Peck Tong)

FOX WISE

A poet has to be a fox
otherwise he will lose
all battles in territory

  for words
    pictures
      ideas
        sounds

and then the bear appears
  from the bush
    the snake
      from the grass
        the wolf
          from the icy plains.

Oh, then the fox
surely has to run
............................for his life!

A fox has to be
  sly and smart

      destructive and kills
      what he likes most
      (e.g. love)

      to be able to create.

FALLEN LEAVES

When I see all these
leaves
on the ground – so many

so confusing

so senseless
reckless

necessary to make
new life
as all things have to die.

I wished my common sense
worked better: when a door
is closing
another door is opening.

Yet I feel the heavy weight
as many seasons go by.

No one knows how it will be
when the last leaf
has fallen in someone's life –

the last word could be anything.
How precious are our days!

(for Jostein Sæbøe)

SEA FOOD

These fruits from the sea
I wonder when nobody
ever touched them
and we still could see them
shimmering on our plates
talking to each other
being happy
a joint venture
of poetry.

I am glad I have my memories
and can picture time back
how you took a fork from the table
and I saw with some respect
you wrapped their shining bodies
in a silver allegory
and I'm perfectly amazed
blurted out some fancy words:
thanks for this! Oysters from heaven.

WHAT GOES AROUND

When you forget about the newspapers
you'll hear other stories

they seem to pop up
from an unknown neighbourhood

like the story about the fake eggs
sold by an old man as genuine

about friends who got mixed up so intensively
with each other
that their marriages went straight to a danger zone.

Today a nurse was telling my husband at his job
that she knew a couple with fifteen children

which is pretty rare these days,
in the 21st century.

Father goes with ten mattresses to the sea
in his car, drops them in a rented house

goes back to pick up half of their children.
Mother has a car of her own and takes

half of their children with her to the sea.
The same thing happens when they go back.

It reminds me of a poem I've read in translation
by which a few words disappeared in the merry-

go-round of the full length of the original meaning
behind which we search nothing but the truth.

WHITE BOAT

You are not gone. You will return
where a boat bobs at a drogue
on calm waves off the coast of Brittany.
You sleep on in the murmuring of the wind

through evening leaves. On a terrace
a man and a woman drink cider
under a parasol, in the sun's slanting rays.
They talk of you, of death, with lilting voices.

She walks across the grass to the tide line.
Her feet leave traces among shells,
dredge seaweed. This searching woman
wades ever further, deeper through shallow

water, not looking back. You are not gone.
She finds you in the bottom of a boat,
bobbing off the coast, lifts you to a dry
spot near the white lighthouses in the distance

on a headland on the horizon where water
in the bay streams to the waters of open seas,
no other distance than a bridge between here
and what has disappeared, that constantly disappeared,

while a man and a woman talk, a table and
a bottle of cider between them. They go on talking
with each other about her, about him, life, the boat,
the sea-bed, the sea that disappears into the night.

(in memoriam of Gerard Rouweler)

BALLET IN THE AIR

On this stormy day
there's a flock of birds
dancing in the air -

they come together on high unseen waves
make turns and fall apart
in deep layers of joy and illusions, and return.

I look around - see people (also myself)
running from one place to the other
often for no reason at all.

Oh - how painful maps and mirrors are
when you discover simple crossroads
of life above your head!

BANJO

My mother was
good on the banjo

She left her banjo
back at the farm
when she married my
father

I have never heard
mother play the banjo

FOX

In the wedding photo mother stands
with that fox round her shoulders

her fur coat
and her showpiece

I look in the mirror
see myself in her
the same eyes, the same hair.

In the middle of summer
I am wearing a dead fox

dark beady eyes
stare unchanged at me:

call it love
but the clasp is missing.

DAUGHTER

for Karin

How beautiful you stand there
leaning against a balcony

in the shining sun. The light
transparent on your blond hair

and I feel you are so far away,
grown out of mother ground

and words to protect you
against all those difficult, high stairs,

obstacles, all what has to do
with growth and pain.

There you are with your
sweet head down, short white skirt

with broad flounces, in Gaudí's Spain.
The world will not drag

you that easily in its trap.
Put the right leg forward.

CHURCH BELLS, WORDS

FRIEND IN SCOTLAND
(about brambles)

I have a friend
he lives in Scotland
the place is Dumfries

it illuminates me in my dark memories
of great lakes
and green hills with naked summits you can see
from a great distance

at the foot a village
with only one bakery, one grocery,
one hairdresser.
Quiet in its shadow.
The moments of quietness, alone with your shadow,
is simply magic.

In the woods grow wild brambles
with sharp thorns. He makes a pudding of them,
he wrote me today –
brambles make a wonderful pudding.

Sometimes I regret living in the low lands,
so far away from my friend with brambles
to be picked freely in September

and on Friday Nights at the Burns Club
a celebration of their patron Saint I don't know either.

ANSWER TO A PUBLISHER
(house, garden and kitchen)

Oh, yes, I clean my house,
windows – mostly on Sundays,
vacuum carpets and make beds
in the morning, or evening

I do laundry, dishes, work
in my garden too,
I draw weeds from the soil,
mow the lawn in the evening

when the sun is almost down.
I rake and I gather my moments
together like participles of gold, dust,
hang them in the sky, my most personal

beliefs, imagination and let the time be
my only judge. Oh, yes I'm quite busy.
Thanks Mr X for your reply saying that
my poems are house, garden, kitchen poetry.

INTERNET IQ TEST

As I was waiting

As I was waiting while my husband
fell asleep on the couch

I drank a cup of coffee in the lounge
of Hotel Comfort Inn

while I was waiting for some news
from somebody from Europe and I finished

the poetry book 'What is Home'
from local poets from Portsmouth.

As I was waiting
for you

I put on a machine and it showed me
an IQ test

and as I remember from my childhood at school
there were a lot of mathematics and circles in it

and square and round shapes with missing links in all colours.
While there was still a war on TV going on in which 9/11 and

the situation in Iraq was compared to Vietnam and the Pearl Harbour
Affair, I thought: maybe a test of knowledge wouldn't harm me

to check on my history brains. But somebody opened the door
and showed me the highway to blue skies, poetry and consciousness

of other matters by which I forgot to finish any test. Moreover,
time is over now and I wait for you and you can drop in any moment.

GRONINGEN

It's quiet in Groningen - I haven't
been there for a long time

I still see before my eyes
people gathering in a square,
a bus pulling up, direction of Noorderplantsoen
while a cyclist bumps against the sidewalk
but that's all there is.

A long time I haven't heard anything - long time
no see - forget and be forgotten,
poetical voices drift away
to the west and the south.

It's so quiet in Groningen that I can hear the wind
creaking in faraway words
and from time to time, in the distance, church bells
from the Martini Tower. No poem

with some sound comes down here
over the dikes of many a river,
while I'm standing with open arms
to track each drowned or lost person.

Though recently it was in the newspapers
that in a village not far from Winsum
the houses collapsed at an earthquake
3.2 on the Richter scale.
This report reached me rather soon.

FATHER

I contemplate my father on his deathbed,
his hands lying motionless on the sheet,
the only movement his shallow breath
and eyes occasionally looking upwards.

Much he endured in the course of this life,
sometimes his struggles took place within
invisible walls, amongst angels, demons,
before he lay down to rest in this bed.

No need to say that I love my father
and tell him that, while there is still time and he
gently squeezes my hands, holding me still here
rather than the opposite. He gives me back the name

I had as a child. Father, go now, just gently go,
go to your much-loved garden at the old house,
or to mother, or your mother, or if need be
to God. Here there is nothing, everything beyond.

THE RECURRENCE OF THINGS

We stood once more at the same point in the wood
with a fence I had once sat on with my sisters

of which there was still a photo from 1967.
Father was in it too, wearing his grey hat.

We walked on, arm in arm, in Sunday harmony over
the asphalt road to the castle of Twickel where families

were lingering. The laugh of a young girl, between
her parents, made the sombre sky brighten.

Dark-brown leaves crunched beneath our feet and the
trees remained silent. With the rhododendrons that would

blossom once more with the advent of spring their buds
would also unfurl into new life even though the earth was

dead, desolate. Our hands fleetingly touched as we realised
we would have to leave something indispensable behind here

if we were to gain new images. All those winters over,
the happiness that comes to you at unexpected moments.

EYE TEST

for Joris

I cover my right eye with my
right hand, read Love Letter

and with my left hand my
left eye, read Love Lace

and at last I know for sure
on your wall it says: I Love You.

Nothing's left in the fog and
nothing foggy drifts as a haze,

a dazzling light, before my eyes.
And when you sit in the bath with me and I've

really removed my lenses, see nothing, then
I still see you clearly before me, even better

when I come closer. Come ever
closer to you in words and water.

NIGHT RIDE

Wer reitet so spät durch
Nacht und Wind…
(Goethe)

for Joris

Perhaps you will remember something
of it. The dancing words

gliding over our faces clung
to lips that were murky but sweet.

Perhaps you still recall that I told you
that later when glass broke in my hands

and I saw nothing more than misty
traces of blood along the side of the road.

It rained that evening, my cases already
packed and the town left in haste as if

I would find you behind a ring road of
meanings. Blood, love, the heavy breath

of an unfulfilled longing. Forever this
once more, once more and always elsewhere

beyond the asphalt of time. The green paths,
the soft light that was to remain with us.

ONENESS

Motionless we lie side by side
a closed book of poems by Yeats

on the floor beside the bed.
We let our hands rest

on stomach and leg. We lower our eyes
and our mouths lapse into silence

in the dark. I entered a wood
because a fire was burning in my head

and you were moonlight. You were
stars, soft earth and fallen leaf.

Motionless we lie together in the night
like raked together fragments of life.

AT A COAST

A fishing boat. Hauled up onto the beach.
Nets lying rolled up on the sand.
The boat empty. The water gone.
Clouds drift on to another shore.

So we lie side by side. You and I.
You went past the table to the window.
You came back. You put papers away.
We became words and flowed together.

AS IF FROM NOWHERE

This morning not seen anything. The trees
laid motionless straight up in their garden bed,
though one cloud – clouds do always
move – drifted in the high sky from the right

to the left side. I still hadn't seen anything.
I waited almost like an old lady – also my veins
in my head don't bow that deeply anymore
to remember this – for you:

the movement. The first act. If you could only
make a pot of coffee. If you could only hold
my hand for a while. Nothing.
Yet unexpectedly brown spots

passed by from behind narrow trees.
Two horses. They had broken away
from the contours of their own existence,
galloped after each other as if on the run

stood still in a corner of the window.
I clearly saw white blazes on their heads.
Isn't the arts the same? First incomplete,
something is missing, and then in full power and rush

like foaming waves hitting a rock.
Like from the tight blue sky the winged
horse never comes alone and carries with him, in his
distant shadow, a ship's gong, the sounds of the gamelan.

PRESENT

Today I bought a bouquet of flowers
for myself

I don't know why

somewhere I had the feeling
that I deserved this

more than my sister's birthday,
the wedding day of my neighbours,
the boy's graduation, or whatever else –

or maybe it was as if this bouquet of marguerites
looked at me in a strange way
in the supermarket,
the last flowers in the bucket to be sold.

The next time I'll just buy flowers
without any thought,
without any effects.

FREE NOTES

on seeing the work of
Eduardo Chillida
(Gallery De Mijlpaal, Heusden-Zolder, Belgium)

To be able to return
you must have been somewhere
outside the well-known circle
and security, mother country,
the familiar voices of people
that only speak your language.

Only then, back on home soil, do you look
differently
your eyes have travelled along with time,
your hands know what love is
in blackness of the ground, whiteness of a virgin
virginity, snow. Lips have burned
for the ferocity of passion
which drags also madness with its desires.

Cities have left their labyrinth traces behind
and from the multiplicity of stripes, forms, materials
a black line has arisen which could have been
different on paper. But it bends
towards a direction at random in a curve, occasional idea,
impulsive and thought over thoroughly such as a poem

after alienation and distance
retrieves the essence sometimes in that one word, image.
It is situated along the border of a map
we cannot point out, and that doesn't exist.

The art of being is for what you chose, white or black, stone
or wood, or both in contrast: the one not without the other.

REQUIEM FOR WORDS

I buried them late in the evening
after many glasses of wine,
a toast to what they meant to me
for the progress I've made in time.

I said: *thank you* not knowing I had ever been
that polite to whatever I knew so well
had crossed my path a thousand times,
which curse is a lasting hang out in hell.

Forgiveness is the best virtue
when you look over your shoulder again,
since what is done is done.

Not a thing can change a buried mind
until it starts all over again
and lifts its hand above the grave.

A WORD IN A STAR

I am not a great star
shining over the black fields at night,
no rivers you'll see flowing
to the other side of the land

but my star shines high in the
dark sky of the northern atmosphere.

You only see the tiny shape of it
in the distance
after many pages have been turned over
in a book written by a holy hand -
the sign is clear and steady.
Only clouds passing by cover

its image now and then. Sometimes
you don't see a thing and it looks
as if everything has gone forever
buried like the ghosts of the past:

it doesn't want to be shown,

but this is all
temporary

as my star is seeking hiding places.

It comforts itself with silence
and the knowledge of the unknown
as the world is old. Older than anything
you can imagine and full of rocks
and other materials at the bottom of the sea.

SUN IN BRANCHES

Already early in the morning –
I don't like young sunbeams in my bed
waking me up –
I found myself in the sounds of Sibelius.

I got up, pulled on my night gown,
and walked barefoot to the lakes
lying stretched out
peacefully in the woods.

I changed into a nymph on a lily,
drifting aimlessly to the water's edge.

I lay down and closed my eyes
as you lay naked beside of me.

Nothing covered our souls.
You disappeared in the pain between
my heart and kidneys
and I blew a clot of blood away which blocked
the passage to your artery.

Together we saw the morning sun rising up
behind thin and bare branches.
In the distance I heard a cello playing
and above it the sound of a violin –
our voices evaporated in each other's mouths.

ROBIN IN PEARSE'S GARDEN

for Pearse Hutchinson

In the front garden of an old house in Rathgar Road
a robin hops through the grass.
It is the robin of Emily Dickinson,
who no one ever saw since she mostly stayed at home
and lived inside walls like the old poet Pearse,

who we're paying a visit one Saturday afternoon in April
in Dublin. The taxi stops at the door to take him
to his familiar pub round the corner, but he no longer
goes there. He no longer goes anywhere, living with
his books and old newspapers

from his beloved Spain, scattered over the floor. I sit in
a low armchair, silent, to let the men talk amongst
themselves. Men who were friends and have always remained so
and who have more to tell each other than women in the kitchens,
in a park. But he looks at me from behind thick glasses

and talks, also with me. He fills his time with talk
of old memories from the 50s, as if it was yesterday.
Joris sits opposite him, one leg slung over the other and listens
to his every word, feels his old body close at hand
like a warm fireplace and what they share is: a feeling,

as he later puts it. A feeling stronger than years and innumerable
visits to an unpainted house where Pearse's mother once used to live.
A robin hops over the grass as I stand outside for a moment
to leave the men to themselves. Men who will always stay true to
each other in friendship, flaws, old bones, old loves, old memories

of old loves, as for a priest on a street in Barcelona,
a fluttering soutane that causes the imagination to swirl up like poems
by Neruda, within reach on the table, that every day cause life to swirl
open when you have nothing more to lose after loss and only own
your soul, your past, a temporary presence of a distant friend close by.

BLACK LOVER

You with your dark gleaming skin of copper
like the horse that every morning I used
to see snorting in my back meadow
in a seam of winter mist
brought to me in the darkest night the deepest
heart of the Caribbean. In every word,
every whisper, I heard the breakers of the sea.
Your gestures, graceful and intense, were so brimful
of gaiety, your eyes shining like stars high in the sky
while in your old Toyota you showed me the outskirts
of the town, the harbour, the dilapidated houses,
the beach with palms, that I wanted to stay with you
for always, in the utter poverty of that deserted island.
I had to go. I had to leave you behind. I had
to feel the pain of loss and boundaries
but when I once more hear the drums and songs
of times long past
you are the one who carries me away,
the one who lets me live, who gives me life.

The poetry of Hannie Rouweler resembles the divine islands of the Archipelago as referred to by the great Hölderlin. Even for those who have never visited them, they are like old friends, one recognises them as if they had just risen from the sea, pure summits of the earth clawing out of the waves, always present, always testifying to what is lasting and real in the magic of a human being working with words.

Mircea Ivanescu (Romania)
(*Calator catre cuvint,*
University Lucian Blaga, Sibiu,
translated by Liliana Ursu)

A poem by Hannie Rouweler is distinctive – it has an individual voice. When reading her poetry, you often get the feeling of changing gear, almost of going into neutral. The mood created by many of her poems is one not of stillness but of stasis – like the stone that has landed in the pond before the ripples come. And the ripples do come – after the poem has been read – spreading outwards from a deceptively calm centre.

John Irons
(Denmark)
(*A timeless tide*)

Among the various emerging voices in Dutch Poetry the voice of Hannie Rouweler is special for the sensible perception of a reality, transferring its concrete aspects to a fugitive and unexpected vision in a serene restlessness.

José L. Reina Palazón
(Frankfurt)
(*Rompiente del día*)

Freshness and directness of the voice.

Chana Bloch
(Berkeley, USA)

There is a consistent and recognizable voice carrying a warm and relaxed tone, but keeping control of the formal handicraft at the same time. It is a pleasure to both the tongue, the ear and the mind to read these poems.

Jostein Sæbøe
(Norway)
(*Lakes and Gardens*)

Demer Press, ePublisher, Belgium

Parchment, Testament, poems by Joris Iven (translator: John Irons), 2008
Lakes and Gardens, poems by Hannie Rouweler (translators: John Irons and Hannie Rouweler), 2008
Mirrors and Deserts/Spiegels en Woestijnen, bilingual, English/Dutch, poems by Anise Koltz and Margalit Matitiahu (translator: Hannie Rouweler), 2008
Anniversary Dinner Robert Burns, My love is like a red, red rose, bilingual, Dutch/English, poems by Joris Iven (translator: John Irons), January 2009
De voorvaderen en de heilige berg/The ancestors and the sacred mountain, poems by Mazisi Kunene, ZULU POEMS, bilingual, English/Dutch (translator poems: Joris Iven; translator Epilogue and Interview: John Irons), 2009
Hommage aan de schilder Tony Mafia/A tribute to the painter Tony Mafia, BLACK SUN, bilingual, Dutch/English, 10 poems/10 poets from The Netherlands and Belgium (translators: John Irons and Annmarie Sauer), 2009
Moving Spots, poems by Hannie Rouweler (translators: John Irons and Hannie Rouweler), 2009
Love as Flowers, poems by Stella Evelyne Tesha, 2009
Mooie rode zijden liefde/Beautiful red silk love, bilingual, English/Dutch, poems by Pearse Hutchinson (translators: Joris Iven and Peter Flynn), 2010
Beroemde Chagga verhalen/Famous Chagga stories, bilingual, English/Dutch, stories by O. Mtuweta H. Tesha (translator: Melissa Yvonne Tesha; co-translator Hannie Rouweler), 2010
Poppies and Chamber Music, Ten poets from The Netherlands and Flanders, editors: Thierry Deleu and Hannie Rouweler (translator: John Irons), 2010
Enlightened from inside out, Poems and Art (translator: John Irons), 2011

website: www.demerpress.be
e-address: info@demerpress.be

www.ingramcontent.com/pod-product-compliance
Ingram Content Group UK Ltd.
Pitfield, Milton Keynes, MK11 3LW, UK
UKHW021820190726
13853UKWH00003B/1082